I0454585

Mastering Mindful Eating
basic to advance

Transform Your Relationship with Eating for a Happy, Healthy, Brain and Memory Loss

By

Katherine Martin

Copyright © Katherine Martin 2024

All Rights Reserved

Table of contents

Introduction

Welcome to the transformative journey of "Mastering Mindful Eating: Basic to Advance." In a world inundated with hurried meals and mindless consumption, this book serves as your compass to a more intentional and fulfilling relationship with food. From foundational principles to advanced techniques, embark on a path that goes beyond diets, focusing instead on the art of mindful nourishment. Discover the power of presence in every bite, unravel the intricacies of mindful practices, and cultivate a harmonious connection between your mind, body, and the food on your plate. This comprehensive guide invites you to savor not just flavors but the profound joy of eating with awareness. Are you ready to elevate your eating experience and nourish your well-being from the inside out? Let the journey begin.

Chapter One

Introduction to Mindful Eating

In the hustle and bustle of our modern lives, the act of eating has often become a rushed and unconscious routine. This chapter serves as a gateway into the world of mindful eating, introducing you to the fundamental concepts that will pave the way for a more intentional and nourishing relationship with food.

Understanding the Basics: Delve into the core principles that underpin mindful eating. Uncover the significance of being fully present during meals, shifting away from autopilot consumption. We explore how mindfulness can transform the mundane act of eating into a rich and fulfilling experience.

The Mind-Body Connection in Eating:
Connect with the intricate interplay between your mind and body during meals. Explore how thoughts and emotions impact digestion and overall well-being. Gain insights into the profound influence of mindfulness on the assimilation of nutrients and the body's response to different foods.

By the end of this chapter, you'll have laid the groundwork for a mindful eating practice, appreciating the importance of being present and attuned to the signals your body sends during meals. The journey has just begun, and the simple act of awareness promises to unravel a world of profound changes in how you perceive and engage with the food on your plate. Are you ready to take the first step towards mastering mindful eating?

Chapter Two

Foundations of Mindful Eating

Developing Awareness in Everyday Meals:
This chapter delves into the practical aspects of cultivating mindfulness in your daily eating habits. Learn to bring attention to the subtleties of each bite, appreciating textures, flavors, and the overall experience of nourishing your body. We explore simple yet powerful techniques to anchor your awareness during meals, breaking free from distractions and fostering a deeper connection with the act of eating.

Cultivating a Mindful Eating Mindset:
Building on the basics, this section delves

into the mindset that forms the bedrock of mindful eating. Discover how to approach meals with curiosity and non-judgment, releasing preconceived notions about 'good' or 'bad' foods. Explore the concept of intuitive eating, where your body becomes the guide, and understand the harmony between hunger, satisfaction, and satiety. This chapter equips you with the mental framework essential for a sustainable and joyful mindful eating practice.

As you immerse yourself in the foundational principles outlined in Chapter 2, you'll begin to witness a subtle shift in your relationship with food. By developing awareness and adopting a mindful mindset, you pave the way for a more profound and fulfilling connection with the nourishment your meals provide. The journey to mastering mindful eating is a transformative one, and these foundational elements serve as the building blocks for what lies ahead. Are you ready to embrace a mindful approach to your meals?

Chapter Three

The Art of Savoring

Techniques for Savoring Flavors: In this chapter, we explore the enchanting realm of savoring – a key aspect of mindful eating. Dive into techniques that elevate your sensory experience during meals. From mindful chewing to paying attention to taste nuances, discover how savoring each bite amplifies the pleasure derived from food. Uncover the link between heightened awareness and a more profound appreciation for the flavors that dance on your palate.

Engaging the Senses in Eating: Beyond taste, this section delves into the engagement of all your senses during meals. Explore the visual appeal of your plate, the aroma of your food, and the sounds associated with eating. Understand how a multisensory approach enhances your overall dining experience, transforming it into a sensory celebration. By the end of this chapter, you'll have a repertoire of techniques to engage all your senses, creating a richer and more mindful connection with your meals.

As you embark on the journey of savoring, you'll find that each meal becomes an opportunity to indulge in a symphony of sensations. The art of savoring goes beyond mere sustenance; it becomes a celebration of the present moment, a practice that transforms ordinary meals into extraordinary experiences. Are you ready to infuse your dining with a newfound appreciation for the sensory delights of food?

Chapter Four

Mindful Meal Preparation

Bringing Mindfulness to the Kitchen: This chapter invites you to extend mindfulness beyond the dining table and into the heart of your culinary endeavors. Explore how the process of preparing food can be a meditative practice. Learn to bring a mindful presence to each step – from selecting ingredients to chopping, cooking, and presenting. Discover how mindfulness in the kitchen not only enhances the quality of your meals but also deepens your connection to the entire food preparation ritual.

Creating a Nourishing Environment: Beyond the physical act of cooking, this section emphasizes the importance of cultivating a nourishing environment in your kitchen. Explore ways to declutter and organize your cooking space to minimize distractions. Understand how the energy and intention you bring to the kitchen influence the quality of the food you prepare. This chapter provides practical tips on fostering a mindful kitchen environment that supports your overall well-being.

By integrating mindfulness into your meal preparation, you not only enhance the flavors of your dishes but also create a harmonious and intentional space. This chapter serves as a guide to infuse mindfulness into the heart of your home, making every moment spent in the kitchen a mindful and gratifying experience. Are you ready to transform your kitchen into a sanctuary of mindful nourishment?

Chapter Five

Emotional Eating and Mindfulness

Addressing Emotional Triggers: This chapter navigates the intricate relationship between emotions and eating, offering insights into the world of emotional eating. Delve into the understanding of emotional triggers that influence your food choices. Learn how mindfulness acts as a powerful tool to bring awareness to these triggers, allowing you to make conscious decisions rather than succumbing to impulsive or emotional responses. Gain strategies to recognize, accept, and navigate the emotional landscape that often intertwines with our relationship with food.

Mindful Approaches to Emotional Well-being: Building on awareness, this section explores mindfulness techniques tailored to foster emotional well-being. From mindful breathing to cultivating self-compassion, discover practices that empower you to navigate emotional states without turning to food for solace. This chapter aims to equip you with a toolbox of mindfulness techniques to create a healthier and more balanced relationship with both your emotions and your plate.

By the end of this chapter, you'll have gained a deeper understanding of the complex interplay between emotions and eating. Armed with mindfulness tools, you'll be better prepared to respond to emotional cues with intentionality, fostering a more harmonious relationship with food and emotions alike. Are you ready to investigate the transformational power of mindfulness in dealing with emotional eating?

Chapter Six

Advanced Mindful Eating Practices

Deepening Mindfulness in Complex Situations: As we progress into advanced mindful eating practices, this chapter explores the application of mindfulness in more complex and challenging dining scenarios. From navigating social gatherings to handling busy schedules, discover how to maintain a mindful approach in the face of various external pressures. Uncover advanced techniques to deepen your mindfulness practice, ensuring that it remains steadfast even in the midst of life's demands.

Mindful Eating in Social Settings: Delve into the art of mindful eating when surrounded by others. Explore strategies to maintain awareness and intentionality in social gatherings, where external influences can often disrupt mindful practices. Understand how to engage in conversations without sacrificing the connection with your food, creating a balance that enhances both social interactions and your mindful eating journey.

This chapter serves as a bridge between the foundational aspects of mindful eating and the more intricate challenges that arise in real-world scenarios. By mastering advanced mindful eating practices, you'll not only strengthen your commitment to mindful living but also navigate the complexities of various social and environmental factors. Are you ready to elevate your mindfulness practice to new heights and maintain your center in any dining situation?

Chapter Seven

Mindful Eating for Health

Understanding Nutritional Needs Mindfully: This chapter delves into the intersection of mindfulness and nutrition, guiding you to approach your dietary choices with awareness and intention. Explore the principles of mindful nutrition, understanding the nutritional needs of your body without succumbing to restrictive diets. Learn to make food choices that align with both your health goals and the principles of mindful eating, fostering a balanced and sustainable approach to nourishment.

Integrating Mindfulness into Dietary Choices: Building on the foundation of nutritional awareness, this section introduces practical strategies to integrate mindfulness into your daily food decisions. From grocery shopping to meal planning, discover how to make choices that not only contribute to your well-being but also align with the principles of mindfulness. This chapter equips you with the tools to view food as a source of nourishment and energy, promoting health and vitality.

By the end of this chapter, you'll have gained a comprehensive understanding of how mindfulness and nutrition intertwine. Armed with this knowledge, you can make informed and conscious choices that support your health goals while embracing the joy of mindful eating. Are you ready to explore the synergy between mindfulness and nutrition for a healthier and more balanced lifestyle?

Chapter Eight

Mindful Eating for Weight Management

Exploring Mindfulness in Weight Loss: This chapter addresses the intersection of mindfulness and weight management, offering a nuanced approach to achieving and maintaining a healthy weight. Explore how mindful eating can be a powerful tool in weight loss journeys by fostering a deeper connection with the body's hunger and satiety signals. Learn to distinguish between physical and emotional hunger, enabling you to make mindful choices that support your weight loss goals.

Sustainable Approaches to Healthy Weight: Building on the foundations of mindful eating for weight loss, this section shifts focus to long-term weight management. Discover sustainable approaches to maintaining a healthy weight without resorting to restrictive diets or short-term fixes. Understand how mindfulness can be a guiding force in creating a balanced and nourishing relationship with food, ensuring that your weight management journey becomes a sustainable and fulfilling aspect of your overall well-being.

As you navigate the complexities of weight management through a mindful lens, this chapter aims to empower you with the tools and insights needed for a holistic and sustainable approach. By integrating mindfulness into your relationship with food, you embark on a journey towards achieving and maintaining a healthy weight while embracing a more profound connection with your body. Are you ready to explore the mindful path to weight management?

Chapter Nine

Mindful Living Beyond the Plate

Extending Mindfulness to Daily Life: This chapter transcends the boundaries of eating, inviting you to weave mindfulness into the fabric of your everyday existence. Explore how the principles of mindful eating extend beyond the plate and into various aspects of your life. From mindful movement to intentional breathing, discover practices that promote a mindful lifestyle. Understand how incorporating mindfulness into your daily routine contributes to overall well-being, fostering a sense of presence and balance.

Integrating Mindfulness into Self-Care Practices: Building on the concept of mindful living, this section emphasizes the importance of self-care as a cornerstone of well-being. Explore practices that nurture the mind, body, and soul, cultivating a holistic approach to self-care. Learn to prioritize rest, relaxation, and rejuvenation, creating a sustainable foundation for mindful living. This chapter provides practical tools to integrate mindfulness into self-care rituals, empowering you to navigate life's challenges with resilience and grace.

By the end of this chapter, you'll have gained a holistic understanding of how mindfulness extends beyond the act of eating, shaping your entire lifestyle. As you integrate mindfulness into various facets of your daily life, you'll experience a profound shift towards greater balance, presence, and well-being. Are you ready to embrace mindful living beyond the confines of the dining table?

Chapter Ten

Culmination: Mastering the Art of Mindful Eating

Reviewing the Journey: In this final chapter, we reflect on the transformative journey you've undertaken throughout the book. Review the foundational principles, advanced practices, and the mindful living concepts explored in preceding chapters. Celebrate the progress made and recognize the shifts in your awareness, attitudes, and relationship with food.

Embracing a Lifelong Practice: As we conclude, shift your focus to the future.

Explore the concept of mindful eating as a lifelong practice rather than a temporary endeavor. Understand that the art of mindful eating evolves with you, adapting to the various stages and changes in your life. Embrace the idea that mindfulness is not a destination but a continuous journey of self-discovery and growth.

This chapter serves as a guidepost, encouraging you to integrate the lessons learned into your daily life. By mastering the art of mindful eating, you've not only cultivated a healthier relationship with food but also fostered a deeper connection with yourself. As you embark on the ongoing journey of mindful living, savor each moment, and relish the rewards of a life shaped by conscious choices and a mindful presence. Are you ready to embrace the culmination of your efforts and embark on a lifelong adventure of mindful living.

www.ingramcontent.com/pod-product-compliance
Lightning Source LLC
Chambersburg PA
CBHW072225290526
45794CB00007B/2890